Meet a Baby Bald Eagle

Heather E. Schwartz

Lerner Publications • Minneapolis

Lerner Publications Company
An imprint of Lerner Publishing Group, Inc.
241 First Avenue North
Minneapolis, MN 55401 USA

For reading levels and more information, look up this title at www.lernerbooks.com.

Main body text set in Billy Infant Regular. Typeface provided by SparkType.

Map illustration on page 20 by Laura K. Westlund.

Library of Congress Cataloging-in-Publication Data

Names: Schwartz, Heather E., author.
Title: Meet a baby bald eagle / Heather E. Schwartz.
Description: Minneapolis, MN : Lerner Publications, [2024] | Series: Lightning bolt books. Baby North American animals | Includes bibliographical references and index. | Audience: Ages 6–9 | Audience: Grades 2–3 | Summary: "Bald eagles are fascinating birds, and baby bald eagles are irresistible! Readers will learn what a baby bald eagle's early days are like, how it eats, and when it's ready to hatch its own eaglets"— Provided by publisher.
Identifiers: LCCN 2022035362 (print) | LCCN 2022035363 (ebook) | ISBN 9781728491080 (library binding) | ISBN 9781728498225 (ebook)
Subjects: LCSH: Bald eagle—Infancy—North America—Juvenile literature.
Classification: LCC QL696.F32 S39 2024 (print) | LCC QL696.F32 (ebook) | DDC 598.9/431392—dc23/eng/20220809

LC record available at https://lccn.loc.gov/2022035362
LC ebook record available at https://lccn.loc.gov/2022035363

Manufactured in the United States of America
1-53039-51057-10/4/2022

Table of Contents

A Baby Eagle is Born

Bald eagle parents take turns in the nest. They protect their eggs. They wait about one month. Finally, baby bald eagles hatch.

For the first few hours, the eaglets are white and wet. After their down dries, they look gray and fluffy.

Baby bald eagles have fluffy down.

Eaglets are tiny next to their parents. Adult bald eagles are 28 to 38 inches (71 to 96 cm) long and weigh 7 to 15 pounds (3 to 7 kg). Eaglets are 4 to 5 inches (10 to 13 cm) long and weigh about 3.5 ounces (99 g). They're the size of a deck of cards.

Adult and baby bald eagles

Nine days later, their down turns darker. They can't fly, walk, or care for themselves. Eaglets need their parents for everything.

Staying Close to Mom

The eaglets' mother stays with them in the nest for the first two weeks. She keeps them safe from predators such as raccoons, crows, and owls.

Bald eagles can spread their wings wide.

She protects them from the weather too. When it's hot and sunny, she spreads her wings to create shade. The eaglets stay cool and comfortable.

By two weeks old, the eaglets can hold up their heads. It's easier for them to eat. They don't need their mother to keep them warm.

Eaglets grow quickly!

By three weeks old, they've grown to about 1 foot (0.3 m) tall. That's about the size of a large bottle of soda.

Finding Food

The eaglets chirp softly in the nest. They want food! They might demand eight meals a day.

At first, bald eagle parents take turns hunting. They bring fish, birds, and other animals back to the nest. The hungry eaglets chirp loudly. Their parents tear off meat for them.

Bald eagle parents bring eaglets food.

Eaglets swallow their food whole. It goes into a storage area under their chin. They digest slowly.

The food storage area in an eagle's chin is called a crop.

As eaglets grow, they rely less on their parents for food.

By about four weeks old, eaglets can stay alone in the nest. Both parents hunt nearby. They bring back food. The eaglets can soon tear meat and feed themselves.

Growing Up

Eaglets gain weight each week. At nine weeks old, they are full size. As they grow, they spread their wings. They catch the wind and float above the nest. The eaglets will soon fly to nearby branches.

This young eagle has caught a fish.

By about twelve weeks, eaglets can fly with their parents. They learn to hunt.

A month or two later, the eaglets go off on their own. They have long lives ahead. They live to twenty to thirty years old.

Bald eagle in flight

By five years old, bald eagles have a white head and bright yellow beak. They look for a mate and start the life cycle over!

Bald Eagle Life Cycle

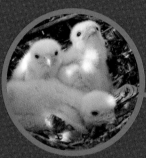

Time until eggs hatch: about one month

Baby bald eagle eats on its own: about five weeks

Fully grown: nine weeks

Life span: twenty to thirty years

Has a white head and yellow beak: five years

Baby bald eagle can fly: twelve weeks

Habitat in Focus

- Bald eagles live in Canada, the United States, and Mexico.

- Bald eagles have excellent eyesight. This helps them hunt prey and spot other bald eagles up to 50 miles (80 km) away.

- During mating season, bald eagles often perch on a branch to sleep. They don't fall off because their feet are made to stay put!

ARCTIC OCEAN

Alaska (US)

CANADA

Hudson Bay

PACIFIC OCEAN

UNITED STATES

ATLANTIC OCEAN

MEXICO

Gulf of Mexico

Bald eagle habitat
Country border
State/province border

Fun Facts

- Bald eagle eggs are the size of a tennis ball.

- Bald eagles can swim.

- Bald eagles pant like a dog when they are hot or nervous.

- The term *bald eagle* comes from the old English word *balde*, which means "white."

Glossary

cycle: a repeating set of events or actions

digest: to change food into forms the body can use

down: soft, fluffy feathers

eaglet: a baby bald eagle

hatch: to come out of an egg

mate: either one of a pair of animals that are breeding

predator: an animal that hunts and eats other animals

Learn More

Britannica Kids: Bald Eagle
https://kids.britannica.com/students/article
/bald-eagle/576747

Harts, Shannon H. *20 Fun Facts about Bald Eagles.*
New York: Gareth Stevens, 2021.

Murray, Tamika M. *Meet a Baby Moose.* Minneapolis:
Lerner Publications, 2024.

National Geographic Kids: Bald Eagle
https://kids.nationalgeographic.com/animals
/birds/facts/bald-eagle

Sommer, Nathan. *Eagles.* Minneapolis: Bellwether
Media, 2019.

Wild Kratts, PBS Kids: "Bald Eagle Nest Rescue!"
https://pbskids.org/video/wild-kratts
/3021264300

Index

Photo Acknowledgments

Image credits: Mark Newman/Getty, pp. 6, 8, 9, 11, 12; Dennis W Donohue/Shutterstock, p. 4; predrag1/Getty, pp. 5, 19; Martin Smart/Alamy Stock Photo, p. 7; Kevin Griffin/Alamy Stock Photo, p. 10; Gerald Corsi/Getty, p. 13; EyeEm/Alamy Stock Photo, p. 14; imageBROKER/Alamy Stock Photo, p. 15, 19; Lea Scaddan/Getty, pp. 16, 18; Pete Niesen/Shutterstock; Josh Miller Photography/Getty, p. 19.

Cover credit: Mark Newman/Getty.